SECOND EDITION
"Principles of an Untapped Mind"

LLOYD LEITCH

Paint Your Own Picasso
"The Principles of an Untapped Mind"
Copyright © 2025 Lloyd Leitch

All rights reserved. This is a self-help book. Any resemblance to any persons dead or alive is purely coincidental. No part of this book can be replicated or duplicated without reference to the book. No part of this book may be stored in a retrieval system, database, and or published in any form or by any means, electronic, mechanical, photocopying, recording, or otherwise, without the prior written permission of the author and or publisher.

ISBN: 979-8-218-64485-7

Lloyd **"Blackstone"** Leitch
Email:
lloyd.leitch@yahoo.com

Cover Design & Interior Design by:
Carlos V. Kaigler/ C'vaughn'K Graphic Designs/ Author The Poet B.GKL
www.authorbgkl.com

Paint Your Own Picasso

SECOND EDITION
"Principles of an Untapped Mind"

FORWARD

"It is not about me. But what is on the inside that defines me."

L. Leitch

INTRODUCTION

As I write this introduction. I am constantly plagued with thoughts of speaking the true intentions of the mind. However, this second addition to **"PAINT YOUR OWN PICASSO: The Ascension of a Positive Mindset."** Shall take a different direction into **"The Principles of An Untapped Mind."** As we explore, the possibilities will guide us along our many journeys to come.

This second edition is unlike the first book. The text of this published piece aims to share my perspectives, and even suggest some useful guidelines. This book offers more of an in-depth side of my wisdom, knowledge, and understanding of how I perceive life, growth, and development. Moreover, my views of the world around me. In the end, these ideas are just my personal interpretations and insights. More so, **"there is no one size that fits all narratives."** The hope is to learn, teach, and heal while influencing future generations on the decisions we make as people living in this world.

FIRST EDITION

PAINT YOUR OWN PICASSO
"Ascension Of A Positive Mindset"

CONTENTS

Chapter 1: Awareness 10

Chapter 2: Change 12

Chapter 3: Resentments 15

Chapter 4: Detox–
Spiritual, Emotional, and Psychological 17

Chapter 5: Growth 21

Chapter 6: Development 23

Chapter 7: Positivity 27

Chapter 8: Purpose & Compassion 31

Chapter 9: Consideration 33

Chapter 10: Mindfulness 37

Chapter 11: A Chance 39

Chapter 12: Unspoken Conversations 41

Chapter 13: Unforeseen Moments 44

Chapter 14: True Colors 47

Chapter 15: Good Energy 50

Chapter 16: Ascension 53

Chapter 17: Staying Focus 55

Chapter 18: Expectation 57

Chapter 19: Embracing Peacefulness 59
Chapter 20: Family 61

About The Author 64

L.B.L

Paint Your Own Picasso "The Principles of an Untapped Mind"

CHAPTER I
AWARENESS

The knowledge or perception of a situation or fact. It can also be a concern about something or a well-informed interest in a particular situation or development. The above-stated definition is derived from the Oxford Dictionary. But let us examine. Awareness from the position of the individual. As human beings, we are born with an awareness. We also have senses that impact and influence this gift. Some may possess 5 or 6 inclusive senses of touch, sight, hearing, smell, and taste.

Other honorable mentions can include proprioception, vestibular sense, and spatial awareness. You can look them up for further details and information. As I think about what awareness means, my mind allows me to rationalize it as an ability to be in tune with the realities of life and the environments in which we exist. We must consistently recognize that our awareness is innate and a **"BIG"** byproduct of our overall success. When we fail to tap into it just pay attention to the meaningful and not the meaningless. Only then are we able to harness our inner power and establish a true sense of balance.

The focus within this chapter is for us as a people to start practicing our awareness. Especially within the things that bring the most positivity to derive a deeper sense of happiness, support, and purpose. Let us start with the things we all know and that are familiar to every one of us. Examples of these are family, life, love, support, and care. I endorse these basic but fundamental principles since they have stood the test of time and reigned throughout the ages.

Paint Your Own Picasso "The Principles of an Untapped Mind"

CHAPTER 2
CHANGE

What is this thing we call or refer to as change? Why does it always affect us? Are we always able to see its effects on us, and on the rest of the world? These are just a few questions that will plague the mind. I can go on asking 1,000,000 more questions about this topic alone. But the only fact that remains consistent and truly probable is that change is necessary. One's ability to facilitate that **'said change'** can be considered another story.

On a further note, and with deeper analysis. The Oxford Dictionary describes. Change. With the use of words or phrases like. To alter, modify, convert, or turn, form, from one state or substance into another. These scientific explanations and examples offer us insights into how change takes place. In my first masterpiece, the focus of change was the establishment of **'The positive mindset'** and then continuing the ascension thereof.

Change is the one thing in our life that directly affects our state or levels of comfortability. It gives us uneasiness, sometimes even an elevated level of doubt, fear of the unknown, and uncertainties of desirable or undesirable circumstances. I think it is fair to say. When it comes to areas of change, all of us may have some underlying hesitations and internal reservations.

This feeling of internal conflict for change is normal. I concur that it stimulates the potential for growth and development. This perspective is often subjected to the person or persons having the experience or experiences. There is an old saying which says the only two certainties in our lives are **DEATH!** And the other, **CHANGE!** Moving forward, let's just use this knowledge to initiate a catalyst of internal change; to work on our mindsets, health, wealth, goals, dreams, and aspirations.

In the end. Let us not only focus on appearance when thinking about change. Be reflective in areas of true character, mindset, and growth. Do not ever change out of force or peer pressure, because this will lead to resentment. Change out of humility, honesty, and out of necessity for growth.

Paint Your Own Picasso "The Principles of an Untapped Mind"

Paint Your Own Picasso "The Principles of an Untapped Mind"

CHAPTER 3
RESENTMENT

Let us start with its definition in Wikipedia, which states that **"Resentment"** also called ranklement or bitterness is a complex multilayered emotion that has been described as a mixture of disappointment, disgust, and anger. Many psychologists consider it a mood or a secondary emotion. Including cognitive elements that can be elicited in the face of insult or injury.

What are the situations in our lives that developed into resentments? Can we identify them? On a deeper analysis, it is indicated by the definition. Most of its initiatives come from external forces. Since external forces are the known culprits, we need to be very mindful of the situations and things that can cultivate these types of emotional unhappiness and/or emotional discomforts. Resentment is the type of emotion that, if left unaddressed, can induce stress, worry, and fatigue in daily relations. Whether as friends, family, or sometimes in marriages.

Resentment can also be burdensome to its carriers. Sometimes it constitutes hyper excessively negative thoughts. It may spiral into other things like anxiety, sleep deprivation, depression, and self-deletion ideas. This type of emotional trigger should always be monitored and kept in check. As a person would you want this type of obstacle to create a domino effect on other things? I beg to differ! The focus as we move through this chapter is acknowledging the importance of identifying our resentment areas or triggers. Finding out better ways or avenues to better treat and deal with our resentments will foster happier moods and more meaningful outlooks.

Different situations and circumstances will test us continually; these experiences may leave us feeling overwhelmed. These states of being can feed resentment. Just remember that this is not the end, every impossible task at times can be made possible. Sometimes all it takes is for us to take the first few steps in getting out of our head. And targeting the source of our discomfort.

CHAPTER 4

DETOX- SPIRITUAL, EMOTIONAL AND PSYCHOLOGICAL.

The definition provided by the Oxford Dictionary states that a detox is a process or period in which one abstains from or rids the body of toxic or unhealthy substances; detoxification.

SPIRITUAL

This type of detox requires us to look deep inside our spirits and spiritual closets to do some house cleaning. We all have some unwanted things within our lives that need our attention; start by immediately dumping them into the trash can of undesirables.

Our spirits are very fragile and delicate and if not properly protected, can sometimes be easily broken by experiences or by people. Some of these include negative frequencies, negative vibrations, and energies. Soul sappers, skeletons in our spiritual closet, (figuratively speaking). Acting as **'A Spiritual GAS Station'** to people, things, and situations we need not be involved with or in… in the first place. Past hurts, struggles, and trauma; detox your life from all of these and watch the transformation begin, your outlook renewed, and circumstances improved for the better.

EMOTIONAL

Emotions, emotions, emotions! We all have them, male and female of the species. It is the ability to control these emotions. For example, anger, lust, jealousy, envy, greed, hatred, love, malice, unforgiveness, etc. These are just a few of our most notorious. Emotions may attempt to govern our outlook and perspective on life. It is my firm belief and understanding that one's emotions should always be held in check. Especially when it starts leaning toward negative and criminal thoughts.

An emotional detox is imperative to ensure peace, balance, and tranquility of the mind. Try your best and hardest, never to become overly emotive, erratic, or sporadic, especially when the situation does not call for it. Emotions are there for us to express what is going on inside, but tact should be considered when doing so. Sometimes it may even indicate something is wrong, a cry for help, aid, or counsel.

Other elements that we should be aware of are **"Emotion Triggers."** These are the set of forces or things that will evoke or invoke certain emotional responses. These triggers are everywhere, and they are all around us. Sometimes popping out of nowhere, being from anything or anyone, igniting impulsive emotional reactions; unnecessarily. These instances are usually uncalled for by the perpetrators and may indicate an inability to control deeper underlying factors. Moreover, I suggest therapy, counseling, or meditation to channel these negative energies out of one's life.

Consider our emotions to be fluid like water or volatile as a raging fire. It is just a **'Pilot of Expression'** so however we fly, the plane of emotion is always dependent on us.

PSYCHOLOGICAL

According to Google's AI, psychological means relating to the mind, mental or emotional, rather than the physical. It can also mean influencing or involving the mind, such as psychological stress or well-being.

Our mental health and our psyche should always be one of the things we need to place on the top list of priorities. When understanding our overall health. A big part of healing Within the structure of health commences with a good sound mind. Our neurological makeup might be fragile but powerful at the same time.

When dealing with the mind and the psychology behind it, it is impossible, not to start thoughts that operate during the thinking process. In doing so, we will have to carefully Identify, analyze, observe, and authenticate. The thoughts, Ideas, and perspectives that flow within the chambers of our heads. The way that we think should always be held in a state of objective; subjection since our thoughts, our mind along our psyche is usually untamed as the tongue. On a deeper level, it is safe to suggest that our mentalities towards anything can sometimes paint a certain picture or open a window to how one's character and personality may, be, viewed or perceived.

We are who we are! not because of our outward appearance. Because of the inner workings of our mind and the psychology behind it. The 'Mind' is like a home and must be taken care of. Moreover, the **'Psyche'** are the persons or the people that live and dwell in that home. It is therefore safe to assume how the overall structure, integrity, and function of that set home. It is truly dependent on the influences, contributions, and maintenance of our psychological thoughts.

I think it should be noted that a psychological detox is necessary daily to ensure that we remain in a position of cognitive clarity. The mind is like a field where a farmer can cultivate abundant produce as he or she wishes or desires. The potential is limitless when decision-making skills are tuned and properly developed. This will inherently correct unpleasant habits and help us navigate the inner as well as the outer workings, throughout our existence.

The **"MIND"** can either be objectively-subjective or subjectively-objective, so govern it wisely.

CHAPTER 5
GROWTH

As I continue my journey on this positive level with a renewed sense of direction and an increase in purpose. I have finally embodied the idea. That nothing in life is without its challenges. We rob ourselves of a unique opportunity to create desirable outcomes when we consent to doubt and fear. Why not consider, instead of focusing on the problem, try to focus on the solution? Instead of holding on to past failures and mistakes. Try resolving, releasing, and letting go.

Sometimes giving yourself a chance in life is all that matters. All that counts, and all that is needed to have newfound confidence. It can even mean a renewed sense of purpose. My first book was truly **"The Ascension of a Positive Mindset."** Moreover, its focus was not about me. But it was the ability to navigate my thoughts, conquer my fears, and keep my mind in check. For if I ever lost the ability to control it... Then what would be the point of anything?

The world of **"Mankind"** has changed a lot since I was a young man growing up. I can remember when the times were different as I moved along, it will continue to change. Remnants of who we were and what we were about. Would become a distant memory long after we all would have departed. This is a known fact as well as death being inevitable but, in the meantime, let us try a little more towards not living like the wild and reckless kind. Instead, practice self-love, self-care, and self-respect, this is key.

Paint Your Own Picasso "The Principles of an Untapped Mind"

CHAPTER 6
DEVELOPMENT

- According to the Oxford definitions, development is a specific state of growth or advancement. It can also mean a new and redefined product or idea.

- An event constitutes a new stage in a changing situation.

- The process of starting to experience or suffer from an ailment or feeling.

These definitions are just a few insights as well as a deeper understanding of development. In this excerpt, we shall address. The one which states an event constituting a new change in a changing situation. Within this analysis, we will first identify two key areas:

1. Firstly, let us look at the development of oneself on a personal and transparent level. As we take a careful look into our being. What are the untouched areas within our lives that are in immediate need of rehab and development? Ask yourself what can I do or do I need to improve on. A very precise place to start would be our thought patterns. How we think can affect our thoughts for development, either positively or negatively. Once we start here. Then everything else will fall into place naturally. Being transparent and truthfully honest with oneself is the most effective way of leading to development. It sets the tone for healing, self-awareness, and self-realization.

Each of us knows exactly the areas within our lives that require work. Furthermore, the challenge is not that. You do not know where to begin, but our procrastination on fixing the relevant and underlying issues. I diligently suggest that we start small when fixing before approaching the more challenging task.

Secondly, we will look at development from outside of our realm of control. In discussing this side of control, here are some familiar topics that become known to us all, they are as follows:

1. **Unforeseen situations-** These can be anything from unexpected bills to family feuds. The range is limitless.

2. **Death-** This is an unfortunate moment within the journey of life. Which usually shapes our perspective. And impacts us in ways unimaginable. With examples ranging from family members, friends, pets, coworkers, classmates, and associates.

3. **Sickness-** In this reality, the possibilities may be as simple as the common cold or flu. Then shift to extreme cases like cancer, HIV, diabetes, and sickle cell. Etcetera. These types of problems come knocking at our doors. When we least expect directly or indirectly.

4. **Divorce and Breakups-** A controversial and overly sensitive issue simply because the remnants of thoughts come bubbling to the surface as we have this discussion. Moving away from Predestine prerequisites that were established in times of old. Set by the foundations of culture, tradition, and practice, are now becoming tainted and watered down to suit a trendier narrative. Hence it is because of this moving away Along with the shift from principles and structure. Separation has become the end goal. I do not think It is the wish of most couples to experience breakups, let alone Become separated through divorce. This direct blow to the family carries a lot of complicated and complex intricacies that should be considered before making any impromptu decisions.

5. **Job Loss-** I decided to add this last Snippet. Since we are all aware of terminations, layoffs, downsizing, etcetera. Job loss Indicates Mental torture and sometimes constitutes a limitation

to our financial flow. It is therefore necessary to make the appropriate decisions for savings. To prevent any financial inconsistency during the untimely event of job loss.

Paint Your Own Picasso "The Principles of an Untapped Mind"

CHAPTER 7
POSITIVITY

This is defined as a practice of being or tendency to be positively optimistic in attitude.

Within life, many situations and circumstances will arise; some of these things may attack from our own personal as well as internal conflict. These usually include underlying issues. For example, trauma, emotional baggage, resentments, unforgiveness, and hurt. To move forward, we must first start on the inside, and then deal with the other external obstacles. To help in combating these struggles, the focus should be on as follows:

- What are the past traumas that I have been holding on to? Or would have even experienced that I may need to release and let go of. To give myself a chance to move forward with my life or my success?

- Emotional Baggage. This overall is still a case-sensitive topic for most people, and one that remains controversial within the psyche. The task is figuring out where the important emphasis should be placed. A good place to start when identifying what baggage, we are consistently tugging around? By reflecting we can sort out the undesirables. Sometimes we need to leave our luggage at the **'International Airport of Life'**, especially when transitioning to the next flight. This metaphorical concept shows that as people. We will all have to figure out our journeys and ways to move forward. As we self-reflect the answers will always come, and if by chance it does not, then you are not truly an honest reflection.

- Resentments. As I discussed this topic. The dictionary defines or better yet, describes it. As a complex emotion fueled by a combination of anger, bitterness, disgust, disappointment, and disapproval. It continues to highlight this as a feeling of

- Reliving an offense that caused injury in the past can be triggered by several things including:

- Being taken advantage of.

- Being put down, dismissed, or ignored.

- Feeling inadequate, overlooked, or unheard.

- Having unrealistic expectations.

Resentments can also lead to feelings of hurt, victimization, and disempowerment. It can also cause people to avoid uncomfortable communication situations. If left on the address. Resentment can become overpowering, toxic, and damaging to trust and love within relationships. It is with much humanity that I honestly endorse the aforementioned explanations. This is necessary since at times my very own thoughts analyzed the direct and indirect impacts of resentments that are usually plaguing one's mind.

In addressing this issue, I hope that acceptance brings about peace. Especially when we target and deal with the underlying resentments. That healing starts from a place of personal conviction to press forward and move on.

- Unforgiveness. This topic to me simply put this one's inability to forgive, release, and let go. We will have to at some point understand that the things or issues in our lives which we choose to carry along create bigger burdens. These hamper growth and retard our elevations. Unforgiveness for a lot of people can be a demon that torments and may have elements of guilt sprinkled in.

- This type of emotional infection, if left to fester, can constitute more psychological stress and in some cases fuel additional physical or health-related problems. We should all take time off each day and identify the areas within our lives where we may harbor **"Unresolved unforgiveness."** The aim is freedom which offers a release of purpose in pursuing things we love.

- Along my journey, I had to take the time to identify, observe, and analyze areas deeply for self-improvement. During this study, I observed that unforgiveness can sometimes have symbiotic correlations with childhood trauma, absentee parents, broken relationships, and many other forms of neglect.

Sometimes these underlying issues require some form of aid, counsel, or therapy. To combat and offer release, comfort as well as improvements to one's quality of life. It is widely recognized that with the intervention of therapy and with constant practice through meticulous effort there can be results leading to the path of growth and success.

- I once heard a statement that said, "You don't forgive people because they deserve it, you do it to give yourself peace." Whether this statement offers my readers a newfound perspective; It is all up to us depending on our state of mind. I utterly understand that it is our lack of knowledge on specific areas within our lives that oftentimes will hamper us. Let us zero in on growth to make more meaningful decisions.

- Today as you read and reflect on this chapter, I hope that we all give **"unforgiveness"** the funeral that it deserves. Looking to our future with a deep sense of freedom in mind, purposeful in clarity, contributing to overall peacefulness of spirit… whatever this means to us all.

-

Paint Your Own Picasso "The Principles of an Untapped Mind"

CHAPTER 8
PURPOSE & COMPASSION

At some point within our lives, we will all be confronted with the question of PURPOSE. Whenever this time comes, it will be vital that we take the time off to study what drives, motivates, or even encourages us to reach and recognize our goals. Our purpose is that **(THING)** or **(SPARK)** which is ignited to give us meaning and show us our destinies. Within the aspect of purpose, there is a certain discipline that needs to be exercised. To ensure that one does not become tyrannical in pursuing their endeavors.

Simply put, we should not allow our ambitions to take us along a criminal, as well as an inhumane path. When we discuss **(COMPASSION)** the reflection of this attribute. Points to look at are areas of care, understanding, empathy, and sympathy. Especially for the sensitive areas which need and even require some form of consideration. As we all take a moment to reflect on the compassionate side of our lives, the question that creates intrigue and arouses stimuli. What can we truly find?

This question is simple: what are the elements of our lives that we feel a sense of compassion for? Is it for people, animals, or situations? Some might even argue saying only a specific circumstance will require us to be compassionate or even exercise it. As I encourage my readers who are reading this book. Do not forget that we are human and the universe has endowed us with certain biological and intrinsic attributes. These unique gifts set us apart from the negative sides of our primal or animalistic traits.

Compassion, therefore, is a part of our social makeup. This is learned from an incredibly youthful age usually inherited from the love and care of our mothers. The wisdom and knowledge of our fathers so we are then able to express it fully when a situation presents itself. Continuing along, let us remember how we give and receive compassion.

CHAPTER 9
CONSIDERATION

As we dive into my perspective on consideration. Let us stop for a moment to ponder on what exactly this thing is that we speak of. Looking at it, my mind is stimulated to say. It is the ability or task to allow a unique perspective, outside of one's understanding of a particular topic or subject. Consequently, consideration is analyzing all factors outside of our thoughts intending to ascertain meaningful solutions or resolve.

Apart from these personal definitions let us look at some familiar mentions:

- **CONSIDERATION WITH FRIENDS**

This type of consideration is usually one that at times may be complicated, complex, and require precision when navigating its intricacies. When we are considering our friends, we must be careful never to confuse the good ones with the bad and deal with everyone. According to their level of authenticity by using foresight instead of oversight.

- **CONSIDERATION WITH/FOR FAMILY**

This is a familiar taste to everyone: **"FAMILY."** They fall into many different brackets: some are good, some bad, some rich, and some poor. Regardless of how they come, they belong to us all. Others make you laugh, cry, or even get you frustrated. But no matter what, within the spectrum of the lineage, there will always exist a unique connection and a priceless bond. Consideration in this aspect becomes a bittersweet symphony simply because our families are not our friends and vice versa. This intricate balance requires attentiveness to prevent any overstepping of boundaries, inconsideration, or the inability to not hurt the feelings of loved ones. Lastly, the defamation of the family's name.

Is there a mere coincidence that a family is referred to as a tree with many branches? **(The Family Tree)** We are all born different and under various circumstances. No one gets to pick who their mother or father is going to be. We all arrive and then we figure out our identity, way of life, and culture. Traditions are handed down; customs are practiced and there is a sense of pride in belonging. With a deep sense of conviction, I said to cherish the people in your life. Especially those whom you consider and give the name family to. Some by blood others by example, experience, and trustworthiness.

- ## CONSIDERATION WITH/IN RELATIONSHIP

In writing this section, I will attempt to address, suggest, and offer perspectives, only from a place of perception seasoned with my limited point of view. This perspective comes from personal observations, analyzing human nature, and attempting to understand motivation. While trying to rationalize the world within my scope. For those who are attempting or are in some sort of relationship with that special someone. The **(consideration)** is a necessary key, this aids in the longevity and validity of the current relationship.

Within this connection exists two different and yet similar individuals with varying personalities. The mission is to eradicate selfishness before it breeds or spawns unwanted chaos amongst the collective. A relationship in a way is a union of collaborative efforts, from its inception towards the commonality of an end goal. When we decide to participate in these endeavors any type of selfish desire, wants and needs will be drastically affected. My overall aim is for words like **"I"** or **"Me"** should be replaced by **"Us"** and "Our." to create cohesion and unison.

In this installment, consideration fosters a deeper sense of reliability, dependability, and trust. Do not look at consideration within the relationship as a burden or use it as an effortless way out of an issue.

Instead, it should be used with maturity, understanding the reality that couples within any relationship will not always agree, even at times upon the simplest of things.

Acknowledgment and comprehension are key elements in establishing honest communication. Also, for the areas where consideration should be given in the first place. Before we continue let us stop for a moment, as I acknowledge an unspoken truth that none of us are truly picture-perfect. Even if at times we somehow convince ourselves of this. Moving along, it is with the awareness of this known fact. We need to take extra time in truly communicating our areas or avenues of consideration, especially when it is given or received.

Consideration in the relationship setting, will require a lot of effort and work for it to have a fighting chance. Forgetting this fact will inevitably bring about consequences, so let us try to at least do a little work within this area.

CHAPTER 10
MINDFULNESS

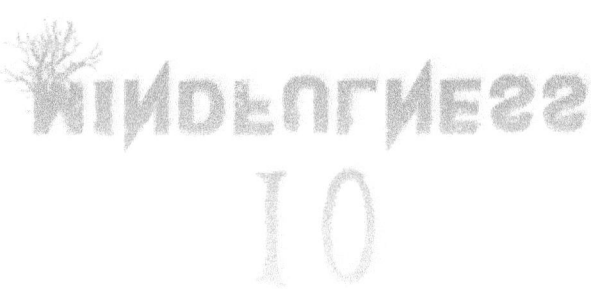

For those curious as to what this is, mindfulness is simply an awareness of one's internal states and surroundings. This is according to its definitions.

Have you ever considered yourself a mindful person? Or are you the type of person who chooses to live life in a state of sheer oblivion? Not being bothered by anything or anyone. These questions are reflective. They implore or even suggest that we ask ourselves. What type of people are we? We live in an extremely disconnected and imperfect existence. This for most can be by choice, design, or control of others.

We are usually unattached from ourselves and the world around us. Linked to the reason that everyone has his or her reason for this type of behavior. Which we all may consider as something duly warranted. Nevertheless, mindfulness in this segment speaks to an area of consideration when dealing with family, friends, and relationships. This requires our best skills of discernment, wisdom, approach, and understanding when dealing with sensitive situations. Am I suggesting that one should take a deep dive into the abyss? No. I am simply saying to assess each situation accordingly while at the same time identifying areas of selfishness, self-centeredness, inconsideration, inability to compromise, manipulations, and deceptive tactics.

Understanding the overall purpose as to why being mindful is necessary gives us the reason we associate, are involved, or are connected to individuals in establishing credible positions. I firmly know that there is a time and place for everything and everyone in this world. Our mission is not to solely focus on everyone's purpose within our lives and lose sight of who we are. This would be a futile endeavor since we have our own lives to fix and focus on, there is much work to be done on both sides. Mindfulness, however, might not be everyone's cup of tea but it should always be considered. When we have young and impressionable minds constantly around us. Believe it or not! We all influence or inspire someone directly or indirectly.

CHAPTER 11
A CHANCE

A chance is defined as a possibility of something happening; to do something by accident or without design; and lastly, the occurrence and development of events in the absence of any obvious design. All of these define and explain… **"CHANCE."**

What is this thing called **"chance"** and what does it mean to you as a person? Does it indicate risk-taking, and stepping into the unknown? Or embracing a level of uncertainty that makes us uncomfortable? When we look at chance within our very lives, it is usually associated with the aspects of risk-taking over everything else. Taking chances sometimes requires skill in decision-making to figure out the right approach for taking a chance on oneself. It is also taking a chance with the uncertainties of a new job/career, relationship, friendship, or marriage.

It is unknown as to what directly motivates us as individuals to take chances in criminal or negative situations. Overestimating one's position to hopefully get a desired outcome. Chances will always be presented on life's table. The menus will always be well prepared with an assortment of various delicacies, appeasing the most seasoned of palates. In these scenarios navigating life's buffet will often require an intricate selection for some type of nourishment. Moreover, satisfying some sort of fulfillment is to be gained. There are many chances as well as opportunities we would have missed.

There are a lot of things we will reflect on, from time to time. We remember the opportunities missed, and thoughts that plagued us concerning the time wasted on entertaining things we should not have done. It is at these moments, that one's disappointments and resentments will come to the surface and sometimes may even carry some form of grief. To be at peace, it is necessary to accept the reality of the chance (s) we took or refused to take. To focus on the more meaningful and important things in life.

Just make peace and move on!

Paint Your Own Picasso "The Principles of an Untapped Mind"

CHAPTER 12
UNSPOKEN CONVERSATIONS

Talking to oneself may come across as weird to many. Are you a self-talker? Or someone who has multiple conversations on different topics and issues with yourself. Do you speak aloud? Or is it just within the chambers of your mind? As I write this bit journey with me let us look at some familiar yet distinct attributes we may possess as human beings. We constantly have dialogue within the inner aspects of our make-up. Some may even have outward monologues that will make the average person look at you crazy. **(Smiling.)** Hopefully, you get the drift.

Regardless of whatever direction one may choose to express these deliberations. It is my sincere understanding that for those who are not labeled, mentally unfit or unstable. This type of unspoken conversations with one's self. Might be a sort of coping mechanism or form of therapy. There are a lot of things within our existence that cannot be explained medically. More so or elaborated upon. As we all live our lives pursuing different paths, I formally endorse having conversations within the foundations of the mind.

My father would often say to me when I was younger that as a man, it was imperative for me to think before I opened my mouth. He would say to me," Son, think before you talk! Your words carry weight so be careful." This has been very instrumental in my upbringing. When making decisions, we must understand that sometimes they not only affect us but our loved ones as well... consider this before any of us can do or say anything. We should run it back in our heads. Double-checking and sometimes even triple-checking just to make sure everything is set or on point. This usually aids in preventing any unwanted catastrophes from ensuing. If you are this type of person there will be a definitive number of results gained through preparation.

Unspoken conversations may be regarded in this context as a form of positive reinforcement. Some may even use it as a type of "Daily-Affirmations." to help deal with other things. As we put positivity out into the universe in whatever we talk about.

Let us remember to be mindful of the creative power within our tongues. Continue to speak, whisper, and mention good things about and over your life. Enjoy your conversations with yourself. Especially if it contributes to happiness, health, and fulfillment then why not?

Paint Your Own Picasso "The Principles of an Untapped Mind"

CHAPTER 13
UNFORESEEN MOMENTS

I chose to write on this topic since there are many unexplainable things that will occur or happen to many of us along the way. Have you ever won a prize? Find money in the streets? Seen someone or a stranger and then had them vanish out of your sight? How about saving someone's life from certain death? These are all examples I refer to as unforeseen moments in our lives leaving questionable thoughts.

The reason behind such events may be very unclear, unknown, or just coincidental. But regardless of their purpose or reason, they do happen to some, if not all, at a given point in time. Another familiar occurrence that is worth mentioning is being in the right place at the right time or being at the wrong place at the wrong time. This type of occurrence can take many forms in different directions given the type of situation.

Here are some familiar occurrences:

1. **Being at the right place for job placement or Immediate on-the-spot hiring.**

2. **Meeting a new or potential love interest because of proximity or impromptu conversations initiated.**

3. **Coming into some form of inheritance, ownership, or business.**

4. **The premature death of a loved one.**

5. **Sickness or disease plaguing the family.**

All of these are familiar examples I choose to classify as unforeseen or unforeseeable moments. Think about being on the Price is Right show and winning the showcase along with the prize money. These incidents carry a degree of luck and chance.

The unforeseeable moments within our lives are the mysterious uncertainties and unknown events that will take place. They may offer a sense of guidance, direction, or even a form of redirection.

Death is also a common participant in the unforeseeable future. Be of good cheer and remember we are here and alive for a reason. Stop procrastinating, do what is right, and do what is of priority i.e., family and experiences.

Paint Your Own Picasso "The Principles of an Untapped Mind"

Paint Your Own Picasso "The Principles of an Untapped Mind"

CHAPTER 14
TRUE COLORS

A song once referenced this. An American singer by the name of Cyndi Lauper. This was her second studio album of the same name in 1986. I see your true colors shining through. Colors carry a deep significance, meaning, and allure. There is also the science behind it, apart from its artistic applications. As we look at true colors within this chapter let us use it as an illustration of human personality. In this analysis, consider friends, foes, families, and familiars.

- Friends occupy a unique place and position relationships within our lives. The separation of sheep from wolves carries much weight; along with the responsibility of ascertaining **(The boundary balance.)** This leaves much room for what is considered acceptable and unacceptable behavior by and from each friend.

- Foes come in many forms, varying in fashions, descriptions, and levels. Some are blatant, deliberate, and upfront, having an uncanny approach. They possess a spiteful view of what they perceive to be success or the totality of your overall life. These types of people are usually chameleons in nature, and it might be difficult to identify them. Use watchful eyes and close observation of every facet of your surroundings.

- Family {**La Familia**} whether by blood or by direct appointment. Some become family because of the value they decided to place on us and the assignments they understood. As they came through for us in ways unimaginable. Hence, we chose to acknowledge them as family. Then we have the most important, 'the Creme de la Creme' which some refer to as the bloodline. Within each bloodline, there exist fractions of the whole where the bonds are unbreakable, controversial, questionable, unpredictable, and unique.

These colors here run much deeper than just names, titles, and the legacies created. The determination, influence, care considerations, and status attained... reflect the magnitude and power of the bloodline. When navigating the true colors within these dimensions only skill, expertise and experience can captain the ship. While wisdom, knowledge, and understanding about life will steer adventurous terrains.

- Familiar falls into numerous categories such as associates, coworkers, neighbors, and people within the community you may know by seeing. Nonetheless, you have no type of affiliation through blood or friendship. They just know you by seeing you and vice versa. Be incredibly careful of all these because some of them may be the shadiest of all colors.

Paint Your Own Picasso "The Principles of an Untapped Mind"

Paint Your Own Picasso "The Principles of an Untapped Mind"

CHAPTER 15
GOOD ENERGY

Have you ever been in a room, space, area situation, or around a person(s) where your entire mood just shifted? Sometimes you feel as if your aura or frequency was disrupted, and your mind is trying to figure out what is happening. Then it is safe to say you will need to be vigilant about the energies you entertain in your space.

Good energy may be a controversial topic for most, but it's the reality surrounding our lives. It can have a greater significance and an impact on our overall health and wellbeing. Consider a person who has a dog, for example. As soon as the owner comes home, the pet rushes to greet them with good energy. Regardless of whatever day its owner was experiencing, the level of love, respect, loyalty, and support remains consistent.

The same type of dynamic can be seen in toddlers or small children as their parents come home from work, they run towards the door with a deep sense of excitement. Awaiting warm hugs and kisses from their parents. In both instances, it is fair to suggest that the parties involved in this emotional display of affection, harness a connection that demonstrates the presence of good energy between the giver and receiver of moods.

This dynamic exchange between the two parties offers insight into the various intrinsic and emotional attributes that highlight the good energy application. Your mood and energy should always be protected. Since it is constantly bombarded or affected by outside forces, these entities are there to change, alter, or adjust your positive aura. Its purpose is to derail your path and obstruct your destination. It is amazing how a good, pure positive attitude along with a healthy mindset can solidify the position of good energy. Good energy often creates a safe space for clarity, vision, and focus.

Many people can attest to things such as a **"gut feeling," "intuition"** or **"having goosebumps."** These types of feelings are usually the most common tell-tale signs most of us will use to measure energies.

Whether these sources are credible or not, the focus should not be ignored. Be aware of your environment and your surroundings. The energy in our lives is there for our own personal growth, development, and benefit. It is a safe house to handle stress, fatigue, frustrations, and any other negative things, especially since we all have mood swings. So, **STAY BEING GOOD TO YOURSELVES...!**

Paint Your Own Picasso "The Principles of an Untapped Mind"

CHAPTER 16
ASCENSION

During our journey on this physical plane, we all at some point may have a desire to be better, in a better position, or situation, or ascend to a higher level. This burning desire comes from intrinsic forces and the need to elevate toward what we consider improvement or betterment. Some may choose to ascend for a form of 'higher consciousness' where there are elements of spirituality, meditation, and enlightenment. This is done in the hopes of finding inner peace and a deeper meaning to life of some sense of balance and tranquility.

Others may ascend because of opportunity, competition, academia, and or corporate goals. The intentions of each individual will always be different from everyone else's. Since everyone is fueled by their specific motivation. Ascension in this segment connotes **"drive."** What are the motivating forces that create life's passions along with the burning desire for achievement? These things are neutral forces, akin to who we are as a people. This deep but strange yearning has its origins established in the workings of our thoughts and the motivations of the mind. The purpose of ascension, therefore should be of good reasons to aid in bettering one's circumstance not only individually but as a whole. It is sad to see that this is not always the case. At times elements of corruption, sabotage, criminal activity, and destruction may infiltrate or try to infiltrate a selected avenue for ascension.

When ascending to any level or height, we should keep in mind the rules of safety. Learning is key and humility is essential. There is an old saying which says. ***"Be careful who you step on the way to the top because these are the same people you will meet or come across on your descent to the bottom."*** So, continue to reach for the stars, but never lose sight of your dreams being distracted by the cosmic dust and asteroids.

CHAPTER 17
STAYING FOCUSED

In a world where destruction is imminent, and tests are inevitable. Staying focused sometimes seems impossible but necessary. Destructions come in many forms in this fast-paced, ever-busy, ever-flowing environment. It can take the form of our careers, family relationships, bills, or expenses. Therefore, it is extremely important that we strategize an effective plan to maintain a level of control. One of a rock-solid nature void of distractions and hindrances.

The meaningful things within the fabric of our lives are not distractions. Some of these include: birthdays, anniversaries, graduations, interviews, and funerals, to name a few. The focus of our discussion is to be able to identify and avoid those idle interruptions, which offer no meaningful purpose, development, or fulfillment. Things like procrastination, and ending up in jail or prison. Getting into stupid altercations more so doing things of that nature. Staying focused is never a leisurely walk in the park. Sometimes it seems the more you try focusing the greater the distractions and obstacles. It sometimes feels as though you are covered by an avalanche of possibilities just lurking in the shadows against you.

Staying focused can be achieved through discipline, dedication, and practice. First, there should be an 'action plan' created with outlined detailed steps. Highlighting how one should go about preparing to have their focus realized. Plan your work and work your plan routinely, and with frequent repetition naturally become a part of you. Over time, practice makes perfect, and the techniques learned usually become second nature. Stay focused always, your survival may one day depend heavily on this.

CHAPTER 18
EXPECTATION

"EXPECTATION" is one of the most exciting, and most dangerous things we will have to come face to face with during our time on this earth. Expectation, simply put, is a belief that something is likely to happen, or something that is expected to happen in the distant future.

Having identified what expectation represents or means, we must ask ourselves what things we are expecting in life and in what areas we may fall prey to this type of thinking. I would like to encourage my readers and audience to be on the lookout for **"unnecessary expectations."** These will usually lay the groundwork for failure. This is the type of expectation that has one's mind unsettled and in a constant state of flux. The intention is usually one in which we might try to navigate our anxiety or worry to bring the mind to a calm.

Hopefully, in doing so we will have the fulfillment of the desired expectation. What am I honestly saying? They may have times as individuals when we may want, desire, or expect a specific thing or certain outcome. There is nothing in the cards of life that states we will have anything just because we expect it. Life requires a little effort from us all in some way. The things which we may expect, are we considering them from a position of logic and reality? Or is it just a whim because of trends? Is it because of desires or emotions? Only you can decide. This is a unique phenomenon synonymous to us all. Showing us how our thoughts work as they relate to expectations. If it is something truly meaningful my encouragement would pursue it for growth and development, otherwise, leave it alone.

Lastly, is it something that leads to your detriment or harm? Will it hurt other people, even the ones closest to you? When looking at our expectations, I ask that we consider impulsive decision-making. Moreover, it is my belief that expectations are neither good nor bad. It is only a 'belief' that needs to be monitored from a position of logic over feelings and probability over possibility.

CHAPTER 19
EMBRACING PEACEFULNESS

"YOUR PEACE IS YOUR RESPONSIBILITY AND NO ONE ELSE'S."

Contrary to widespread belief, true inner peace can only be established from within. External influences of peace are usually short-lived. The expectations of peacefulness as people usually have the tendencies of negative influences, tyrannical behavior, destruction, and death. Embracing peacefulness is usually a decision on an individual level, or it can also be established by a collective group.

This type of mindset establishes the grounds for unbreakable intentions, which serve to prevent disruption amongst parties uniting for a common cause, good, or goal. Let us observe embracing peacefulness from a personal approach. We all have things and thoughts unresolved which may torment, fatigue, and frustrate us all the time. What do we do about it? Do we sit there and allow ourselves to be constantly consumed by worry, anxiety, and hatred? Fueled by past atrocities, inconveniences, and inconsiderations. We all have the choice to release, let go, and move on from the things that are keeping us in a mental hamster wheel.

I decided years ago to make a conscious effort of embracing a peaceful mindset. Not because of the many physical, psychological, spiritual, and emotional benefits. Moreso, not because I saw myself better than anyone else by gaining or obtaining a newfound superpower. I did not figure out some sort of ancient secrets to life and immortality that would have contributed to any type of financial gain or influence. It was because I utterly understood that I was not perfect; I was still a work in progress; and I had a powerful desire to grow, learn and develop. Embracing peacefulness is something that is enriching. We must try our best to find and fix the peace in each of our lives that was stolen. As we aspire to greatness, we will have to first fix within ourselves before looking outwardly.

Paint Your Own Picasso "The Principles of an Untapped Mind"

CHAPTER 20
FAMILY

First, let me start by saying I love my family. The good, the bad, the ugly **(figuratively speaking)** and the indifferent. For most of us, this statement is particularly challenging. I say this with much conviction, understanding that leadership is by example. So yes, I genuinely love my wild, crazy, impulsive, smart, courageous, selfless, selfish, boring, anxious, loving, caring, and influential family.

I do not think that your family is supposed to be perfect. They are just supposed to be there for each other. Not like the fairy tales and movies we see on the television of perfect families. They are supposed to be there for each other not like our parents, but to embody the principles of love, support, guidance, direction, experiences, and presence. I believe every family struggles with diverse types of issues, dramas, and challenges. The beautiful thing that sets each of them apart is their resilience to overcome adversity, fight through the storms, resolve conflict, and establish grounds for a moral compass.

"Before coming into this existence, we were not allowed the chance of picking our families that we would be born into and that is ok. Life gives us the opportunity to always create a family that we would like to have."

L. LEITCH

I think it only fits closing out **(The Principles of An Untapped Mind)** with family because these are the people who play an extraordinarily strong, important, and vital part in our lives. From our conceptions and throughout our lives they will continue to be there in future generations even after we have departed this world.

Be your best, do your best, and forget about the rest. Love, Peace, and Wellness to all.

Paint Your Own Picasso "The Principles of an Untapped Mind"

"What you hear is an opinion, not a fact, and what you see is a perspective, not the truth."
Marcus Arelius

Paint Your Own Picasso "The Principles of an Untapped Mind"

ABOUT THE AUTHOR

Lloyd Leitch is a thought-provoking inspirational writer who gave us **"Paint Your Own Picasso The Ascension of a Positive Mindset."** This book was a deep dive into the reality of life.

Now with **"The Principles and Untapped Mind"** be prepared to transcend your negative thoughts into a purposeful positive-based approach with useful insights and guidelines.

Lloyd "Blackstone" Leitch